JUST TELL ME HOW DAMMIT!

How to Get Everything You Want in Life!

HOW TO GET EVERYTHING YOU WANT IN LIFE

THE STEP-BY-STEP METHOD TO BECOME ANYTHING YOU WANT TO BE...

Table of Contents

Introduction

'How to Get Everything You Want in Life'

That sounds like a pretty lofty title and a rather big goal. Is it really something you can accomplish? Can anyone really get everything they want from life?

What does that even mean?

When you compare most people, you'll find that everyone has different goals with diverse intention. Some of us are trying to change the world and others just want to settle down and be healthy and happy with a loving family.

Then there are those people who want to *fly*.

Can they all potentially get what they want from life?

Of course, speaking imprecisely some people may pessimistically say no and I would optimistically say **yes**.

I think that once you read this book, you'll realize that a lot more is possible than you previously thought. Sure, some of it is about getting a better understanding of what it is you want and some of it is about making do.

But for a huge number of goals, you'll find that the same kinds of principles apply time and time again. There's a 'formula' you can apply to any aspect of your life in order to achieve the things you want to achieve and to be a success – and I'm going to share that formula with you now. By the end, you should be much closer to achieving what it is that you *really* want out of life and to understand where you might have been going wrong in the past.

In this book, you'll learn…

➢ How to identify the things you *really* want from life and then find the easiest way to achieve those things
➢ How to stop waiting for 'life to happen' and to start taking the things you want from it
➢ How to create a business plan that you can execute at any time of your life to achieve incredible things
➢ How to improve your health, your home life, your looks – all with a few simple changes
➢ How to learn to be happier with the things you already have and to value those things that bring you most pleasure

Ready to start living the life you always wanted? Then keep reading!

CHAPTER 1 - KNOWING WHAT YOU WANT

Chapter 1: Knowing What You Want

The first step to getting what you want is *knowing* what you want. This is something that all too often gets overlooked and all too often it's assumed that we already have this.

How many motivational posters tell you things like 'go after that one thing that makes you truly happy!' or 'never give up on your dreams!'? That's all good and well if you've always wanted to open your own restaurant, or if you've dreamed of having your own successful band…

But what if you don't *know* what you want from life? What if you have lots of different interests that are all pulling you in different directions? What if you're like my friend who is a pilot who has always dreamed of flying long haul, but who has a family back home who he'd never get to see?

In these cases, telling someone to 'seize the day and live [their] dreams' just isn't all that helpful!

What you need to do then is to prioritize and you need to look for the things you can get from life that will make you happiest and tick the most boxes.

Let's look at some of the ways you can do that…

Look for the Common Themes

Very often, what this comes down to is identifying the commonalities in your dreams and objectives. In other words, if you want to be twenty things, then what do those twenty things have in common?

If you want to be an actor *and* you'd love to be a rock star, then what is it about both those things that makes them appealing? What does being a rock star have in common with being an actor?

Most likely the answer is that both put you in the public eye, both are a kind of performance and both bring a fair amount of wealth. So as long as you can tick all those boxes, you should be happy *whatever* you do.

The Five Whys

Another way to get to the bottom of what it is you really want and to discover *why* you want it is to use the 'five whys' technique. Here, you ask yourself the question 'why' five times in a row in order to dig deeper and deeper into your motivations.

> *So let's say you want to be a famous novelist…*
>
> *why?*
>
> *Because you want to create something that you can be proud of.*
>
> *Why?*
>
> *Because you want to leave some kind of lasting mark.*
>
> *Why?*
>
> *Because you respect and admire creative individuals who have done the same.*

8

Why?

Because they can make a living by entertaining using only their imagination and their writing skills.

Why does that appeal?

Because you love to be creative and to be acknowledged for that creativity.

Okay, *now* we're getting somewhere!

What you've learned is that perhaps it's not being a novelist specifically that appeals so much as being able to be creative and to get credit for that creativity.

This then opens up a huge selection of different potential career options: now you could be a comic writer, you could be an artist, you could work at a creative design agency… You can get what you want in a different *way*.

Likewise, if you still dream of being an astronaut, then you might find that it's actually the sense of discovery and pioneering that appeals to you. Being a researcher can actually bring about this same buzz and excitement even though you're sitting right at home! Ultimately, you're still being the first person to discover something exciting.

Look to Your Role Models

Another way to find out what it is you really want is to look at your role models and to see what it is about them that you admire. What parts of their lives would you like to emulate? Again: what do they have in common?

Look Back

Another tip is to look back at what you wanted to be when you were younger. Sometimes this will have no bearing – we can change an awful lot in a few decades – but in other cases you'll find that whatever it is you wanted to be back then still has some kind of appeal for you. Back then, you likely dreamed of being something much more ambitious and less 'realistic' because the cynicism of adulthood had yet to sink in. Does that same thing still excite you though? Once again, you can then start thinking about what it is *about* that thing that appeals and how you could realistically achieve the same end.

Considering the Reality of What You Want

Of course this can all still be tricky. Even once you start to uncover the route of what it is that drives you, you can still find yourself struggling to make a choice and to decide on one course of action.

Another thing that can really help then is simply to think about what your objectives will actually mean in *real* terms. At the moment we've been focussing somewhat on career paths and we'll stick with that for the moment. The thing to recognize here though is that the career path you think might bring you the most satisfaction and sense of accomplishment *may* not be the one that actually leads to you being happy.

What do I mean by this?

Well consider for moment the idea of being a high flying executive of a huge corporation. This is an idea that a lot of people find very appealing *until they actually live that life.*

Here's the thing: being an executive of a high flying business means constantly getting phone calls during your home life, working late hours and dealing with highly stressful clients. The actual *lifestyle* will only appeal to a certain type of person.

This is where the concept of lifestyle design comes in. We'll talk about this more in future chapters but suffice to say, lifestyle design means choosing a job to suit the lifestyle you really want, rather than choosing a lifestyle to fit around your job. Want to work fewer hours? Then don't become a CEO! Again, think about what it is about being a CEO that appeals and them mimic *that* without changing your lifestyle. There are plenty of ways you can do this: for instance it might be the idea of wearing a suit and feeling important that appeals to you – both things you can achieve in other ways that don't require quite such a big commitment.

So don't just think about what you *think* will make you happy – actually imagine the day-to-day result of achieving your goals and whether *that* makes you happy too. If you're having difficulty defining the kinds of lifestyles and things that make you truly happy then another option is to think about the times in recent memory that you were happiest. If you can think back to the last time you felt really great, this may well be a good way to identify the kinds of situations and lifestyles that make you happy.

Another consideration is what you want to achieve and what you want to be remembered for. And there's another mental exercise you can use to work this out, which is to try writing your own eulogy. Sounds a little morbid right! Well actually, it can be a great way to remind yourself what's really important and to get your priorities straight.

The idea here is that you write your own eulogy as though it were being written by someone else. However, you're writing it in an alternate universe where your life panned out *exactly* the way you wanted it. What do you want the speech to say about you? How do you want to be remembered?

Some people will want their eulogy to focus on how they were a great family man/woman. Other people will want to be remembered for their great works. What's going into your speech? What really matters to you?

Prioritizing

As mentioned, we've been focussing a lot on career at this point – but that's really only a small part of getting what you want out of life. At the same time, you also need to think about things like your health and fitness, your family life, travel, your confidence. There's a *lot* that makes up a happy and healthy individual.

Classically, you could relate this to Maslow's 'Hierarchy of Needs' – a psychological theory that looks at all the things humans require to be happy. This includes the following:

- Physiological needs
- Safety
- Love/belonging
- Esteem
- Self-Actualization

So at the bottom of these needs you have things like food, sex, safety, shelter. In the middle you have love, belong and self-confidence. And at the top you have self-actualization which relates to your accomplishments and your ability to feel as though you're contributing something, creating something, doing something that *matters*.

This is an old theory and somewhat arbitrary but generally it's true that you need to satisfy both some basic needs *and* some larger goals in order to truly be happy.

But you can't change all these things at once. You aren't going to become a world famous athlete overnight while at the same time fixing your wardrobe and your self-esteem. Likewise, focussing on any career at the same time as developing a successful love life is going to be harder than doing either one of those things on their own.

So in other words, the point is that you need to prioritize what you want out of life and you need to focus on *one* aspect of your lifestyle to begin with.

This means looking at what is most important of course. But it *also* means looking at what will allow you to get the 'quick win'. In other words: how can you very quickly start making a difference? As we will see later on, this is very important. Making some kind of change that impacts you in a real way is important because it will give you that positive feedback that encourages you to carry on making *more* changes and developing your life further.

Look for something that has the best balance of being quick and relatively easy to change *but* also being impactful on your life in a big and meaningful way.

This will all take some time so don't rush it. Sit down with a piece of paper and a pen and hash out what you want from life, what makes you happy and what you can realistically change relatively easy about your current situation. Once you have that thing: act!

CHAPTER 2 STOP WAITING - TAKE ACTION NOW!

Chapter 2: Stop Waiting – Take Action Now!

Of course just creating a list of things you want to change and knowing a bit more what it is you want from life is only a very small first step in getting there.

Now you have to actually start making things happen for yourself and that means taking small, positive steps toward achieving your new goals.

This is where most people go wrong. Not because they go about achieving their goals in the wrong way (though this happens) but because they don't go about it *at all*.

The big problem for many of us is that we're seemingly 'waiting' for something to happen. We're happy to just go along with our current lifestyles which are 'good enough' rather than aim for something bigger and better.

Sometimes this comes down to fear. Sometimes this comes down to thinking they have no other option. Sometimes it comes down to believing that waiting is legitimately the best strategy for getting what they want.

The ultimate example of this is retirement. How many people do you think live their lives cautiously because they're saving for retirement? How many people put off going on holidays and travelling the world because they think it's better to wait for that pay off?

But when you think about it, this makes no sense at all. Of course it makes sense to plan for the future but why would you defer your happiness until you're at a point in your life where you're not physically capable of enjoying it to the fullest? Why wait until you have no energy and a painful knee and spine before you start travelling the globe? It just makes no sense when you *could* take action now and start having the things you want immediately.

Instead, you could start seeing the world *now* by taking sabbaticals or just by prioritizing your travel on your experience rather than spending money on other things or saving as much. Don't wait for that perfect moment – do the things you want to do *now* and live the life you want to live!

Another example of this is wealth. A lot of people will dream about the things they want from life when they're wealthy. How many times have you imagined your perfect home that you will buy when you're rolling in cash? It's something most of us have done at some point.

But now think about what that perfect home actually entails. Most likely, it's a fairly standard property but with the added bonus of looking cleaner, more spacious and more luxurious.

Does it need to be huge? Does a huge house really make you happier? Probably not.

So instead of waiting until you're rich to have your dream home, how about thinking how you can make your *current* home into your dream home? Take action *now* on the things you want!

How to Turn Your Current Home Into Your Dream Home

Let's take this moment to look at how you can turn any property into a dream home on a modest budget. This will hopefully then serve as a good example of how you can get what you want from life much more easily once you've narrowed down what you *really* want.

In this case, you say you want to be rich, but what you really want is a beautiful home. You're putting off doing it because you think that that requires you to be wealthy or retired but you *can* have it right now if you just focus on the small differences that will make that property feel closer to the one in your dreams. Here are some steps you can take:

➢ Throw out a lot of your things – This might sound surprising but the more of your things you throw out, the more items you'll be left with will start to look beautiful and amazing. If you have a lot of clutter in your home, then you're essentially lowering the average value and the average quality of the things you *do* own. Throw out 90% of your ornaments and the remaining 10% will be the most amazing looking things you have. Likewise, they'll look less cluttered and thereby draw more attention to themselves. They'll also be much easier to clean!

➢ Go more minimal – In general, going more minimal with your décor can help you to make your home look much bigger *and* it makes it that much easier to clean. It's also a very modern look that's much more affordable. So stop spending lots of money on large collections of items you don't need and instead save up for just a few beautiful things.

➢ Prioritize! – If it's your home that gives you the most pleasure then how about prioritizing it and spending a bit more money on it right now? That might mean cancelling your television subscription for instance and putting that cash into a cleaner, or it might mean not going on holiday this year and getting double glazing instead.

➢ Learn décor – This is a big one. Instead of just placing items around based on what you think looks good, spend some time *learning* what makes great décor. Once you learn the tricks, you can take a relatively standard looking room and make it look incredible. Does your room have a color palette? Do your cushions match your drapes? It sounds silly but these practices have developed over years of research and business and they make a huge difference.

➢ Look for bargains – If you know where to look and you leverage your contacts, you can make some amazing additions to your home relatively cheaply. This may mean that you speak nicely to your friend who happens to be a builder (mate's rates!) or it might mean that you look on freecycle to find free furniture.

➢ Get a few center pieces – Just a few high tech pieces of technology, or a few amazing decorations can make all the difference to your home. Depending on your priorities that might mean adding a massive flat screen TV to your living room, or some kind of spectacular water fountain. This bit is expensive but it's all about investing your money wisely – making the biggest impact with the fewest changes. And sometimes it's just about doing something *different* that people don't see all that often. This makes your home memorable and it doesn't even have to be expensive.

Suddenly, that home that you thought was off limits starts to feel a lot closer. Sure, it's a compromise, but while you work on becoming that millionaire you'll be *much* happier with the property you're in. Stop deferring your happiness, ask what you can do *right now* within your means to be happier!

The same kind of approach can be applied to your dress sense (just a few clever changes can make your outfits that much more impressive) and to your lifestyle.

In the next chapter, we'll be looking at some of the ways you can start making real progress in your career *now* instead of waiting for something to change for you.

How to Get Both Things

On a final note, you'll find that sometimes the things you want are in contrast to one another.

Remember that scenario we posited at the beginning of the book? The pilot who wants to fly long haul but doesn't want to leave his family?

Actually, it's more complicated than that. What he really wants is to fly for British Airways (he's in the UK) because that gives more status than his current position at EasyJet. Moving there and flying long-haul would be the next logical step in his career but it also means upending his family (as British Airways don't fly from Manchester where his wife wants to live) and it would mean spending long times away from home.

Logically it makes sense to stay where he is – especially as the salary is just as good.

But his heart is telling him to take BA for the excitement of moving forward in his life.

So what does he do?

Of course there's no right answer here. Whatever he does will mean choosing *one* thing over another and sacrificing some aspect of his ideal lifestyle.

What do you in situations like these? Often the answer is to try your best to *do both*.

How in this case can you possibly do both?

Well, one answer might be to move to BA for a couple of years and fly long haul then, only to subsequently give up the long haul and settle down with the family.

Another option could be to move to a third airline – such as Virgin. Here, he'd still get the status and he'd still get to fly further but he would be able to live in Manchester still

And maybe he doesn't fly long haul but he flies *further* than Europe.

As you can see, there are almost always compromises when you're torn in two directions. Wherever possible the answer to 'either or' should be 'both'.

Chapter 3: How to be Anything You Want to Be...

In terms of your career, you can genuinely be anything you want to be. Now you know what you want to accomplish with your life, actually doing that is *easy*.

No seriously.

Want to be a writer? Great, all you have to do is to start writing a book.

Want to be an artist? Sure, just start painting!

Want to be a pilot? Start looking for pilot courses.

Want to be a pilot but can't afford the course/don't want to give up your current lifestyle? Then look into flying a microlight.

The point is that as soon as you start doing the thing you want to do, you *become* that thing. As soon as you write, you *are* a writer by definition.

Sure, you may not be famous for it. You might not be professional. You might not even be any good. But you *are* a writer!

And when someone asks you what you can do, you can legitimately say 'I'm a writer'.

Hopefully what you're getting from this is that you don't have to define yourself by your career. Likewise, you don't have to have just one career. And your finances don't have to be completely tied to your income either.

Again, it's about not waiting. And it's about realizing what it is *about* the thing that makes you excited and happy.

How to Become an Actor or a Rock Star in Your 40s... or 80s! While Supporting a Family

So let us say you always wanted to be a rock star. Now you're in your 40s and you work in logistics. Boy, did something go wrong somewhere or what! This is what mid-life crises are made out of.

First things first: remember the old adage that 'it's never too late to be what you always wanted to be.' That's genuinely true you know. Sometimes it's actually *easier* to accomplish things when you're older.

Always wanted to be an actor but now you're 80? There is *tons* of work for older people to play extras or small parts on TV and as you get older you'll have more time to audition. You can achieve that lifelong dream now! Always wanted to live in LA but now you're 70? Never was there a better time!

Back to being the rock star wannabe with the mid-life crisis. What do you do?

Simple: you start performing music in your garage, you create a home studio on whatever budget you have and you put together a band if you're so inclined. You might be in logistics but you can get your sense of direction and accomplishment from the music. You're not a rock 'star' yet but you sure as heck are a rock *musician*. That's a pretty good start…

Next up, how about creating a YouTube channel for your music? How about uploading some tracks to Sound Cloud or Band Camp? You might just find you get a little following. You might even make a little money.

And there was no risk, no big change in your lifestyle... You're now living that dream! You're a very small rock star and that's good enough.

So the only question is: what took you so long?

Coming Up with Strategies

In that last example we looked at how you could gain exposure for your rock music by using YouTube. The web actually makes all kinds of things possible today that weren't before. Did you know that you can self-publish a book on LuLu and you don't have to pay *anything* upfront? It's called 'POD' or 'Print On Demand' and that means that the copies only get made when they're sold – meaning there's no upfront investment and no risk.

Even before the internet though there have always been multiple ways of achieving the same end. Take a look at Sylvester Stallone. Here's a guy who always wanted to be an actor but no-one would give him the time of day because of his slur.

So instead of giving up, Sly changed his approach. He wrote the killer script for Rocky and then showed that to producers. They were so blown away by what they were reading that they were willing to agree to almost any terms in order to secure the rights to that script. Sly's demand? That he would be the star. The rest is history!

The point is, that you don't always have to go about reaching your goals in the traditional or obvious manner. Almost always, there are other ways you can go about achieving the same thing if you just take the time to come up with a strategy.

What are your strengths? What are your current resources? Who are your most valuable connections? How can *you personally* achieve that goal you have in mind?

Gradual Improvement

Remember too, the longer you work at something, the better at it you become. This applies not only to obvious skills but also business nous and the ability to self-promote. In other words, you might start playing music in your garage and *really stink*. But if you keep at it long enough you'll get better and better until you're close to rock-star-good.

Likewise, if you keep on practicing at the music, you'll eventually get to the point where you learn how best to gain exposure and to promote yourself. Keep at it long enough and success is almost certainly going to be around the corner.

This is also just one more reason to step on it! The sooner you start trying, the quicker you'll get to a professional standard!

CHAPTER 4 - THE STEP BACK TECHNIQUE AND SPRINGBOARDING

Chapter 4: The Step Back Technique and Springboarding

In the previous chapters we've looked at how you can potentially achieve incredible things by changing your approach and by looking at which elements are most important for you. We've seen, among other things, how you can achieve practically any career goal just by using the right strategy to get there.

Here's one strategy then that can work for almost anyone, regardless of their goals.

It's called 'springboarding'.

What springboarding means, is that you're creating success in one area that you can use to create success in another.

So let's say that you want to be that rock star but you aren't sure of your ability to get there using conventional means. What could you do instead?

Well how about creating a website that is highly successful on the topic of rock? Once you get enough people reading the site you'll have a huge audience that you can get direct exposure to. Now all you need to do is to start featuring your own music on the blog and there you have it – a great way to get people to listen to your music.

Likewise, how might you go about achieving what Stallone achieved today? One option could be to create a popular YouTube channel showing yourself acting. Get enough follows and use high enough production values and eventually someone will come knocking with an opportunity.

Another option of course is just to get rich. If you want to make a music video, then all you need to do is to become successful and wealthy in any other area and then you can use the money and the connections from that success to fund your pet project.

Is it vein?

Sure.

Is it a good investment?

Maybe not.

But it makes you happy. It's what you want. It's how you're going to self-actualize. What could possibly be a better way to spend your money?

Creating a Muse

If money is very often the enabler that you need to start being happier in your life, then the new strategy might become to *quickly* increase your income to get to where you need to be. This might sound a lot easier said than done but actually there are once again techniques you can use to make things a little easier.

Tim Ferriss for instance describes something called a 'muse'. This is basically any quick and dirty little business that he can use to start generating passive income. Remember what we said about your main salary not needing to define your wealth?

The easiest muse is often to sell an affiliate product online. This means advertising an eBook or something similar and getting paid commission (up to 75% in some cases). We won't go into how this works in depth here but a quick search on Google will show you that there are plenty of resources that will help you out.

There are other ways to quickly increase your wealth without getting promoted to CEO as well. For instance, how about looking into working on day each weekend in a small job? It's not terribly fun but if it's to fund a dream then it might well be worth it!

Alternatively, you could rent out a room on AirBnB, or you could even let students stay in your property – you can get paid a good amount for this!

In other words, it's key to recognize once again that your salary is not the only source of income. You can even make a lot of money just by saving better and forgoing some of your current expenses.

Do you drink a coffee on the way into work? That can cost as much as $3-$4 in some cases. SO that's now $15 a week or $60 a month. You could be $60 a month better off just by kicking that caffeine habit!

Again, this is all about sitting down and recognizing what your priorities are in life. You're probably doing a whole lot right now just because you've always done it. It's time to change that and to start aiming towards the goals that will actually make you happiest.

The Step Back Technique

The step back technique is a technique that involves thinking about what you want to get from life if you had all the possible resources and success in the world. If *even the laws of physics* were yours to bend, what would you accomplish?

Nothing is off limits here. Maybe you'd like to be a superhero? Maybe you want to save the world and cure the hungry? Maybe you want to be the next Bill Gates.

Write this down and then apply the 'step back technique'. That means asking yourself what the closest thing you can possibly accomplish is.

You'll be surprised at just what you can manage...

You Can Fly!

The title of this book is how you can get *everything you want*.

Right at the start we pointed out that this is a rather lofty aim. Can you really do *anything* you want to? Even if you want to *fly*?

Well the answer is yes: with caveats. At this point in the book, we've discussed enough strategies and techniques that you can now understand why this is the case.

The first thing to do is to look at the reasons *why* you want to fly and what it is about flying that appeals to you.

Is it the speed? Because in that case, you could drive fast cars.

Is it the actual physical feeling of flying itself? Is it the ability to soar through the clouds? Because in that case you could become an airline pilot like our friend, or as previously mentioned, you could learn to fly a microlight.

But what if you want to really fly. *Really fly* without any machinery.

Man, you're going to make this difficult aren't you?

Well in that case, you could use the step-back technique. What's the closest you can possibly come to flying like Iron Man?

There's always zero gravity. So there's that…

Or you could become Iron Man. Iron Man is the most realistic superhero who can fly, we can probably agree.

Still completely impossible. But more realistic.

So step back again. What's the closest you could come to creating a real-life Iron Man suit?

Well, a few people have asked themselves that very question.

There's actually a guy who built himself a 'real-life Iron Man suit' that works using a rocket attached to his back. It can't take off from the floor but if he's dropped out of a plane, the combination of the wings and the rocket are enough to allow him to fly/glide through the air until the fuel runs out. Woah.

And there's another guy who invented something similar. This one allowed him to fly with his hands and feet using thrusters – just like Iron Man.

How? Simple: it only works over water. And instead of shooting out lasers (or repulsors for the real Iron Man fans out there) this suit worked by shooting out *more water*.

In other words, the device takes water from a hose that's submerged into a river or lake, and then it blasts it out powerfully from the hands and feet. It's called the Jet Lev.

Don't believe me? Look it up on YouTube! And if you want to use it you can – there are experience days that let you fly using the Jet Lev!

So you can't be Superman but you can come surprisingly close if you're willing to change your strategy and focus on what it is you really want.

This also applies to other aspects of your life such as your health. If you have a chronic illness then the sad reality is that you might never become an athlete.

But apply the step-back technique and you may realize that you can become a *Paralympic* athlete. Or perhaps that you can get into the best shape possible and do lots of research and become an inspiration to others who are in the same position.

So you may not always be able to become or do anything. But what you *can* do is to make steps towards any dream. And as soon as you start taking those steps, you'll find that this is what gives you that sense of purpose, of satisfaction and of actualization.

CHAPTER 5 - FEAR SETTING AND MITIGATING RISK

Chapter 5: Fear Setting and Mitigating Risk

Now there's a fair chance that many people reading this are going to think it all sounds great, nod their heads a lot... and then just completely disregard it and never do any of it. Unfortunately, most of us won't make the changes necessary to get what we want out of life.

But I don't want that to be the case for you. I want this book to be different – I want this to be the book that makes you actually start making those changes.

And to that end, it's worth trying something called 'Fear Setting'. This is a concept that once again comes from the very wise Tim Ferriss and his book *The Four Hour*

Workweek – which will make for some excellent further reading.

So what is fear setting? Essentially, this is a tool that you use to overcome your fears by making them more concrete. It is the *opposite* of goal setting as instead of writing down your goals, you're going to write down all the things you're afraid of.

So let's say that you think you want to become a self-employed entrepreneur. It sounds great on paper but you're afraid. Here's why:

> You might fail and be humiliated
> You have a family to support – what if you can't get your job back
> You don't have any funding for your idea
> Now is not a good time – you've just had a child
> Your wife might leave you
> You might end up homeless and alone

So those are some fears and some worst case scenarios. Suddenly your dream doesn't seem so appealing.

But wait! Now what you're going to do is to go through each of those points and a) score them out of ten in terms of likelihood then b) write down how you would cope in each situation. Be honest and realistic.

- ➤ You might fail and be humiliated – 7/10
- ➤ You have a family to support – what if you can't get your job back – 6/10
- ➤ You don't have any funding for your idea – 10/10
- ➤ Now is not a good time – you've just had a child – 9/10
- ➤ Your wife might leave you – 3/10
- ➤ You might end up homeless and alone – 1/10

Sure, you can't argue with the fact that you *have* just had a child (though whether or not it is a 'bad time' is debatable). Likewise, you either do have money or you don't.

But it's not that likely your failure will be *humiliating* as such. Likewise, your wife would have to be pretty harsh to leave you – give her more credit than that! And you certainly won't end up on the street. Apart from anything else, you probably *will* get your job back. Worst case scenario you might have to take a less good job, or go begging to Mom and Dad/the government. Not ideal sure, but you would survive.

Now we're going to look at how you cope with any of these things happening and how you're going to mitigate the risk thereby making it even *less likely* to happen.

- ➤ You might fail and be humiliated
  - o You actually don't need to tell anyone that you're trying. Likewise though, why does it matter what people think? At least you tried! And you never have to give up, you can just change your strategy so there's no 'failure' to report.
- ➤ You have a family to support – what if you can't get your job back
  - o As mentioned there are plenty of options here: go for a worse job for a while working in a supermarket if necessary, get benefits, ask your parents for help. Even make money from your own entrepreneurial efforts.
  - o You can probably survive on your savings for a few months at least.
  - o But more to the point – there's no need to quit your current job at all! If you want to set up a business then all you have to do is to set it up on the side by doing it at weekends and in the evenings. Eventually

41

you'll get a good idea as to whether it's going to be a success or not and only *then* do you quit your job. Zero risk involved!

➢ You don't have any funding for your idea
  o Most business models can be 'bootstrapped'. In other words, you can create a model that starts with no investment necessary and then reinvests that money into other projects as it grows. For instance, a website is free to create and the money you generate can then be reinvested into inventory for that ecommerce store you dreamed of.
  o How about Kickstarter?

➢ Now is not a good time – you've just had a child

There is *never* a good time. If you wait for all your stars to align then you'll never do anything.

Would your child rather you were wealthy, or happy?

➢ Your wife might leave you

This won't happen. But if it does then she probably isn't the one for you anyway. Seriously, if you can't do the thing that makes you happiest *and* be in that relationship then you won't be happy.

But it can certainly help to sit her down, to tell her how much this means to you and to show her your plans in detail.

> You might end up homeless and alone

Again, not going to happen. But if it does... Then you'll pick up the pieces and try again! You can crash on a friend's couch in the meantime, or work online to earn enough for a hotel.

The point is: the worst case scenario is not normally as bad as you think it is and there are almost always ways you can cope.

And anyway, what's more frightening: those things happening and you living a full and interesting life? Or you remaining in a job you find soul destroying and boring for your whole life? Not taking a risk is the only way to guarantee that you won't be happy. So take the risk!

This fear setting can be used in all kinds of situations too. This is true whether you're going to be approaching a girl/guy in a bar or whether you're going to be asking your boss for that raise.

A common fear with asking someone out is that they might say no. So how can you mitigate that risk?

Try this: smile at the person from across the room first and see how they react. If they smile back then you have a good chance of them being receptive to your approach. But if they look away, then you've been 'rejected' in a way that had no repercussions and wasn't at all embarrassing. You mitigated the risk!

When you get good at this, fear setting is something you can do automatically in your head every time you're approaching a challenge or a decision that you find nerve wracking. This is actually a basic form of CBT – or Cognitive Behavioral Therapy.

CHAPTER 6 – HOW TO WRITE GOALS

Chapter 6: How to Write Goals

Once you have your strategy in place and you're committed to following it through, you'll then find that the next step is to break what you have planned down into steps that can then become goals.

So your intention is to become that rock star taking our YouTube route? Great. You now have a series of steps:

> Get a guitar
> Create a home studio
> Start a band
> Upload videos

Boom!

The next step is actually sticking to this strategy and executing on your goals.

And this is where we start looking at other aspects of life too, such as dating or getting into shape. If those are your priorities rather than your career, then you can skip the 'coming up with a strategy' part and go straight to the 'following the steps' part.

The difficulty at this stage and what causes many people to fail, is creating goals that are simple to follow.

If you want to get into great shape and have a bodybuilder's physique for instance, then you might have written a goal along the lines of 'lose 3 stone by next year' or 'add 1 inch to my biceps by three months'.

These goals are terrible. No offence.

So what's the problem specifically? It's that the objectives are far too vague and far too distant.

If your goal is to lose 3 stone in a year, then starting today you have a *long* time to accomplish that. This means that you can very easily put off going to the gym or have a cheat day with your diet and still expect to complete your goal.

Which is great, but it doesn't create much incentive to work your hardest.

Likewise, once you get to the end of the year and you've only lost 1 stone, you can end up feeling very deflated and even depressed, causing you to give up. This is a big shame seeing as you've actually done very well losing that much and made a great start!

The other problem is that this goal is so out of your control. What if you work *really* hard and you eat right and train right and you don't lose the weight? This can very easily happen!

So how *should* this goal look?

Try this one:

"I will work out for 30 minutes at least 3 times a week"

Now you have a goal that is:

➢ Simple
➢ Immediate
➢ Completely within your control

Working out 30 minutes 3 times a week is something that is non-negotiable. There's no 'I'll do it next week' this is a simple weekly fail/succeed case.

And if you do fail? Then you just jump straight back on the train the next week.

Another goal might be:

"I will eat no more than 2,000 calories a day"

This is a goal you can accomplish every day. You can stay focussed and you get that great sense of achievement each time it goes right.

But if you wait long enough, this 'micro goal' will add up to help you achieve what you want. You focus on the mechanics, on the cogs turning and eventually you'll *be* where you want to be.

The same goes for those YouTube videos. Now your goal might be:

"Upload two YouTube videos a week"

"Make each video/song better quality than the last"

Making a Chain

Apparently, Jerry Seinfeld uses a technique called 'making a chain' in order to stick to goals like this one.

Simply, he marks an 'X' on his calendar each time he achieves his goal. Eventually, he begins to create a long chain of Xs representing a successful week of accomplishing his aims.

And the thing is, that this is a *very* motivating feeling. It's odd but once you have a long row of Xs, you'll often find you'll work really hard to avoid breaking that chain! Try it yourself and see if it motivates you that little bit more.

CHAPTER 7 - KAIZEN AND CHANGING IT ALL AT ONCE

Chapter 7: Kaizen and Changing it all at Once

Now we're looking a little more at some of the other ways you can move towards your goals by improving your health and fitness and maybe making a start on your love life.

And it's useful at this juncture to point out that it often makes sense to do as many of these things as possible. While we did say that you should have some kind of 'focus' in your objectives, it's also important to recognize the interconnected nature of your life and how hard it is to approach any aspect of your lifestyle in isolation.

What do we mean by this?

Well, let's take getting into shape as an example. If you want to get into great shape and build lots of muscle, then you may be thinking about starting a new training regime working out four times a week.

That's great. But if that's all you're planning then it also won't work.

Why? Because think about it: right now you probably come home from work and feel exhausted. That's probably the reason *why* you're not already in great shape. You're probably pushed for time and have a ton of commitments and your work likely stresses you out.

And now you think you're going to add four hours of intense exercise on top of that?

And not only that, but you'll probably need to travel to and from the gym and you're also going to need to shower. It just won't work and most likely you'll give up by week two. This is what happens to countless people.

One solution to this is to just work out the right way and to train in a way that enables you to get the most benefit from the minimal work. Fitting your training in around your lifestyle also helps – train in the morning for instance and you might only need one shower.

But a better strategy? That's just to *change everything*.

Changing everything means that you're going to look at how you can get more time in your evenings. This may mean:

> ➢ Finding a better way to commute
> ➢ Working from home some days (discuss this with your boss)
> ➢ Changing jobs!
> ➢ Quitting one of your after-work activities
> ➢ Going to bed a little later and lying in a little longer
> ➢ Saying no to friends occasionally

In other words, it's prioritizing again. It's making *space* in your life for this training you hope to do.

Meanwhile, you also want to combat that tiredness. That might mean:

> ➢ Improving the quality of your sleep (new bed?)
> ➢ Reducing stress (at work perhaps, or by keeping your home tidier)
> ➢ Getting more vitamins and minerals in your diet

You'll also find that creating a space to work out in at home makes a difference which means you'll need to do some home improvement as well. As you can see then,

you're no longer just changing one thing… you're
changing *everything*.

The Law of Attraction
This doesn't just apply to fitness and exercise. If you want
to do better in your career, then changing everything makes
sense too.

Being in better shape will help with your career by making
you more confident and more physically imposing.
Dressing better will help with your career. Having more
energy *certainly* will!

Here you can consider the law of attraction. This states that
like attracts like and that if you act in a certain way, your
life will change to match. Act confident, dress well, look
great and people start taking you more seriously. Thus you
start to get given more responsibility and your career
improves. Again then, it pays to make changes in all areas
of your life in order to facilitate improvement across the
board.

Kaizen
If you're the cynical type then at this stage you might be
wondering how precisely you're supposed to go ahead and
'change everything'. Not exactly straightforward!

Well, one answer is employ a technique called kaizen. Essentially, kaizen means making lots of small changes in order to add up to *big* differences in your life. Kind of like the way you bring down a great oak with lots of small chops, or how you can walk a hundred miles by taking lots of small steps.

In this scenario though, we're talking about making lots of small tweaks to your lifestyle and your current situation in order to achieve massive things across the board.

For instance, simply making your bed in the morning is a great little change you can make that will go a long way. Why? Because you'll feel much more organized and much better when you come home to a clean bed and this makes you feel more productive. It's also a great exercise in self-discipline and if you can do this one thing then you'll find it's much easier to stick to your *other* goals.

Cutting out the coffee to save more money is an example of kaizen too (what other small changes could you make?), as would going to bed ten minutes earlier be. Ten minutes is nothing but it's over an hour more sleep every week!

How about investing in a robotic vacuum cleaner/ A small thing for sure but it makes a big difference when it means your home no longer looks dusty and you never have to waste time on cleaning!

CHAPTER 8   WHAT IS 'LIFESTYLE DESIGN'?

Chapter 8: What is 'Lifestyle Design'?

Lifestyle design is something we mentioned briefly in an earlier chapter but it deserves a bit more attention of its own.

To recap, lifestyle design means choosing the job that will give you the lifestyle you want. That means *not* assuming that your job needs to dictate the lifestyle.

For instance, if the main thing you want out of life is to spend more time with your family and your needs are modest, there's no reason that you can't work as a trash collector. When you do this you'll be spending less time working and you'll be home when your kids get back from school. The work isn't terribly stressful (in as much as you don't bring it home with you) and while you might not find it rewarding you can get your actualization elsewhere with your rock band project, your painting or your great novel.

If your main desire is to travel, then you might want to consider working online which will allow you to earn money from anywhere in the world. Otherwise there are plenty of jobs that will facilitate the opportunity to travel. Or just look for somewhere with a good salary and particularly generous holiday/flexible working time.

The Digital Nomad

The ultimate expression of this is possibly the lifestyle of the digital nomad. This is someone who works online and is constantly travelling. They take a laptop with them and find cheap accommodation and they spend most of their time working in a cool bar, or while relaxing on the beach.

Of course the digital nomad will sacrifice a lot of their creature comforts – this isn't a lifestyle that will suit everyone! However, for the right kind of person this really is a dream way to live and it just goes to show what's possible!

Don't be Afraid to be Different

Working online isn't the only way to use lifestyle design. It simply means thinking about how your job is going to affect your day-to-day lifestyle and then picking the right job on that basis.

And yes, this may mean doing a manual job that lets you get fresh air and exercise. Or it might mean doing a job like rubbish collection that lets you work better hours.

But the problem people have with this is that it's not what they're used to. Too often we feel like we need to live a certain lifestyle in order to live up to what's expected of us or to be 'normal'. Even if you'd be *happier* as a rubbish collector, you might go ahead and become a doctor to keep your family happy or to feel as though you're a success.

As you can imagine – this is a mistake and your happiness is what should come first.

Likewise, you also shouldn't be afraid to be a little unusual. Maybe you want to combine careers in a way that's not particularly common and that onlookers would find strange… that's fine! Don't be afraid to be the first. Once again, the fact that you're happy is what really matters.

Chapter 9: An Introduction to CBT

Finally, we'll touch once again on CBT.

CBT stands for 'Cognitive Behavioural Therapy'. This is essentially a framework that you can use to try and improve the way you think and to thereby improve a number of beliefs and behaviors. This uses a combination of practicing, testing and assessing your own thoughts in order to attempt 'cognitive restructuring'.

CBT also teaches mindfulness, which has a number of different applications. One particularly interesting use for mindfulness though is to help increase your own sense of gratitude for what you *already* have. This is very important – if you aren't able to appreciate the things you have already and what you have already achieved, then you'll find that *nothing* you accomplish brings you any closer to being happy and fulfilled.

So make sure you spend the time to think about the things you're grateful for in life and the things that you've already done well. Some people find small exercises like listing three things they're really thankful for each morning can really help. Try doing this and always remember that wherever you are right now in life – there are probably people who would love to be in your shoes.

The CBT Process

As mentioned, you can also use CBT as a great tool for overcoming fears and for generally changing the way that you think about things.

While there are many different aspects to CBT, there is a basic process that most people can follow to start achieving more things and feeling more satisfied with their accomplishments.

Step 1: Mindfulness

The process starts by being mindful of your current thoughts and reflecting on what you currently think on a regular basis. Which thoughts are destructive and potentially holding you back? What can you do about that? Mindfulness can be used as a form of meditation, while you can also use journaling which simply means writing down the thoughts as they come to you or at the end of the day.

Step 2: Thought Challenging

This is the process of challenging your beliefs and thoughts – just like we did with the fear setting process. Does your limiting belief really have any merit?

Step 3: Hypothesis Testing

Better yet is to simply *test* your hypothesis. Think you can't speak in front of that crowd? Think that you'll get laughed at if you ask that woman/man out? Then try it! What you'll find is that the reality is never as bad as you were worried it might be!

Step 4: Affirmations

Believe it or not, affirmations and mantras *can* work when they're well chosen. Repeat phrases that undermine the negative ruminations in your mind and eventually they can completely replace those beliefs.

Conclusion: Keep Moving Forward!

And there you have it.

Sure, you might not yet be raking in the cash and living in a mansion with a beautiful wife/husband. Nevertheless, you hopefully are much closer to living that life – if it's the one you want!

The key is to stop looking at things as so black and white and to look for alternative ways to achieve what you really want. That means identifying what it is you really want out of life and it means coming up with a great strategy to help you get there.

It also means that you stop waiting until you retire or you win the lottery and you look at making as many changes as you can *right now* to get to where you want to be.

You won't get everything you want from life right away of course. But if you keep working at it you'll be highly surprised by what you can accomplish.

And what's more, is that you'll have the rewarding feeling of working towards something. This is often what most of us want most of all – a feeling of forward progression. As long as you're working toward being a rock star, being the best health of your life, being the perfect family man/woman… then it's not just a dream. Having a plan and having a trajectory makes life that much better so it's time to start making progress. Don't stagnate, keep moving forward!

__The following pages are for you to__

__journalize your goals and progress__.

1. Dream it.
  ➤ Write down your Vision, Dreams and
    Aspirations.

_____

_____

_____

_____

_____

_____

_____

_____

_____

_____

_____

_____

_____

_____

_____

_____

_____

_____

_____

_____

_____

_____

_____

Dream it.

Dream it.

_____
_____
_____
_____
_____
_____
_____
_____
_____
_____
_____
_____
_____
_____
_____
_____
_____
_____
_____
_____
_____
_____
_____
_____
_____
_____
_____

Dream It

_____

_____

_____

_____

_____

_____

_____

_____

_____

_____

_____

_____

_____

_____

_____

_____

_____

_____

_____

_____

_____

_____

_____

_____

2. Research it.
> ➤ Research your Vision, Dreams and Aspirations and bullet-point priorities.

_____

_____

_____

_____

_____

_____

_____

_____

_____

_____

_____

_____

_____

_____

_____

_____

_____

_____

Research it.

Research it.

Research it.

3. Create it.
> Identify and bullet-point the goals in each step that would lead to accomplishing your Vision, Dreams and Aspirations.

_____

_____

_____

_____

_____

_____

_____

_____

_____

_____

_____

_____

_____

_____

_____

_____

_____

_____

_____

_____

Create it.

Create it.

_____
_____
_____
_____
_____
_____
_____
_____
_____
_____
_____
_____
_____
_____
_____
_____
_____
_____
_____
_____
_____
_____
_____
_____

Create it.

_____

_____

_____

_____

_____

_____

_____

_____

_____

_____

_____

_____

_____

_____

_____

_____

_____

_____

_____

_____

_____

_____

_____

_____

4. Define it.

> ➤ Define and bullet-point what needs to be done first, second, third… regarding moving specific goals forward for example writing in this book and planning could be considered the first step.

Define it.

77

Define it.

_____

_____

_____

_____

_____

_____

_____

_____

_____

_____

_____

_____

_____

_____

_____

_____

_____

_____

_____

_____

_____

_____

_____

_____

Define it.

5. Visualize it.

> ➤ There are visualization / motivational techniques where upon you imagine yourself accomplishing your vision. The brain is an incredible piece of machinery and if you research and put into practice this tool of visualization, it will help keep you focused and accelerate success.

_____

_____

_____

_____

_____

_____

_____

_____

_____

_____

_____

_____

_____

_____

_____

_____

_____

_____

_____

_____

Visualize it.

Visualize it.

_____

_____

_____

_____

_____

_____

_____

_____

_____

_____

_____

_____

_____

_____

_____

_____

_____

_____

_____

_____

_____

_____

_____

_____

_____

_____

Visualize it.

6. **Journalize It.**
> ➤ Do not forget to write your accomplishments down no matter how small.
>
> What are your accomplishments?

_____

_____

_____

_____

_____

_____

_____

_____

_____

_____

_____

_____

_____

_____

_____

_____

_____

_____

_____

Journalize it.

Journalize it.

_____

_____

_____

_____

_____

_____

_____

_____

_____

_____

_____

_____

_____

_____

_____

_____

_____

_____

_____

_____

_____

_____

_____

_____

Journalize it.

7. Put a line through it.

> ➤ I know you have spent a lot of time building your visions, goals and lists down; however crossing them out when you have completed them is a great feeling.
> Have you completed any of your tasks or goals?

_____

_____

_____

_____

_____

_____

_____

_____

_____

_____

_____

_____

_____

_____

_____

_____

_____

_____

_____

Put a line through it.

Put a line through it.

_____

_____

_____

_____

_____

_____

_____

_____

_____

_____

_____

_____

_____

_____

_____

_____

_____

_____

_____

_____

_____

_____

90

Put a line through it.

8. Stay Focused on it.

> ➤ Persevere through the negative outcomes and set-backs. Allow others to view your work and accept input. Be resourceful and seek refreshment of your vision through new research. What can you re-boot or re-fresh to keep you on task?

Stay focused on it.

Stay focused on it.

_____

_____

_____

_____

_____

_____

_____

_____

_____

_____

_____

_____

_____

_____

_____

_____

_____

_____

_____

_____

_____

_____

_____

Stay focused on it.

_____

_____

_____

_____

_____

_____

_____

_____

_____

_____

_____

_____

_____

_____

_____

_____

_____

_____

_____

_____

_____

_____

_____

_____

_____

9. Know your value and differentiate yourself.

➤ Highlight your outstanding traits and skills. Uniqueness attracts-no matter what your task may be. What is your uniqueness?

_____

_____

_____

_____

_____

_____

_____

_____

_____

_____

_____

_____

_____

_____

_____

_____

_____

_____

_____

_____

_____

_____

Know your value and differentiate yourself.

_____

_____

_____

_____

_____

_____

_____

_____

_____

_____

_____

_____

_____

_____

_____

_____

_____

_____

_____

_____

_____

_____

_____

_____

Know your value and differentiate yourself.

_____

_____

_____

_____

_____

_____

_____

_____

_____

_____

_____

_____

_____

_____

_____

_____

_____

_____

_____

_____

_____

_____

_____

_____

Know your value and differentiate yourself.

_____

_____

_____

_____

_____

_____

_____

_____

_____

_____

_____

_____

_____

_____

_____

_____

_____

_____

_____

_____

_____

_____

_____

_____

10. Reaffirm the purpose.
> ➤ Keep it fresh in your mind. Reaffirming your purpose is powerful. What is your visions purpose?

_____
_____
_____
_____
_____
_____
_____
_____
_____
_____
_____
_____
_____
_____
_____
_____
_____
_____
_____
_____

Reaffirm the purpose.

Reaffirm the purpose.

Reaffirm the purpose.

Maintain passion through rereading this book and repeating the last 10 steps.

Achieving goals, no matter how small they may seem can be life altering. Knowing that with each drop of success comes a flood of accomplishment. If you maintain your enthusiasm and commitment to persevere through the tough times and practice self-discipline you will be successful.

Made in the USA
Lexington, KY
13 February 2019